BONES

SKELETONS AND HOW THEY WORK

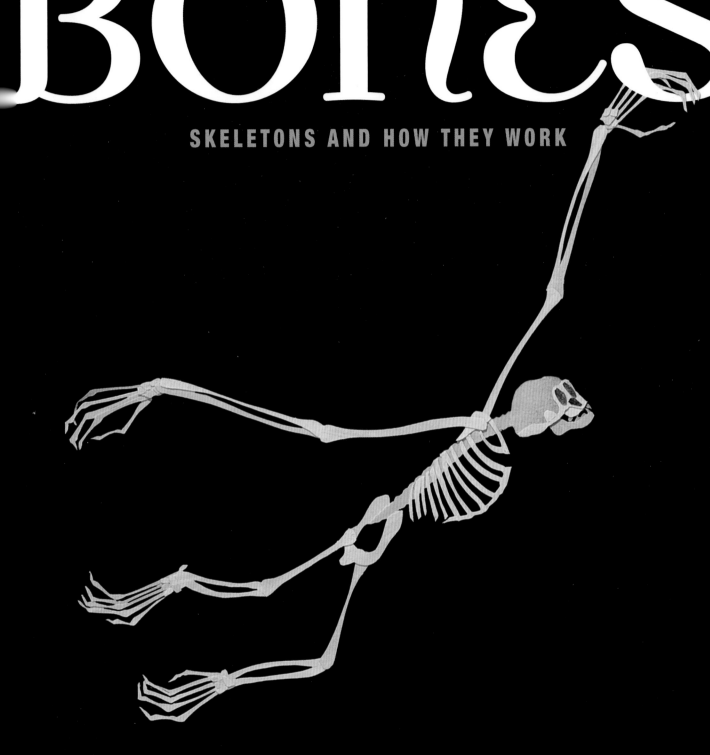

STEVE JENKINS

SCHOLASTIC PRESS • NEW YORK

GIANT ANTEATER SKULL

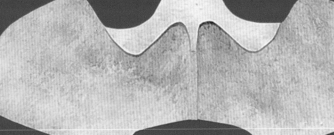

TURTLE PELVIS

DOG RIB

HUMAN
FOOT BONE

ALLIGATOR SHOULDER BLADE

Large Bones, Small Bones

HORSE THIGH BONE

AARDWOLF
JAW

BARN OWL SKULL

Bones, Bones, Bones

Bones are alive. They grow as an animal grows, get stronger when they are strained, and repair themselves if they get broken.

The bones in an animal's body form its skeleton. The skeleton provides support, protects the brain and other delicate internal organs, and allows an animal to move.

Mammals (including humans), reptiles, amphibians, birds, and most fish have bony skeletons. None of them, large or small, could survive without bones. Remove an animal's skeleton, and it would become a helpless, squishy sack of skin.

Bones, like the animals that depend upon them, come in a wide range of shapes and sizes. Every bone in the body has its particular place and job to do.

Where do you think this bone belongs?

That's a Handful

This is one of the bones inside a human finger.

There are a total of 27 bones in a human hand.

Add three more long bones . . .

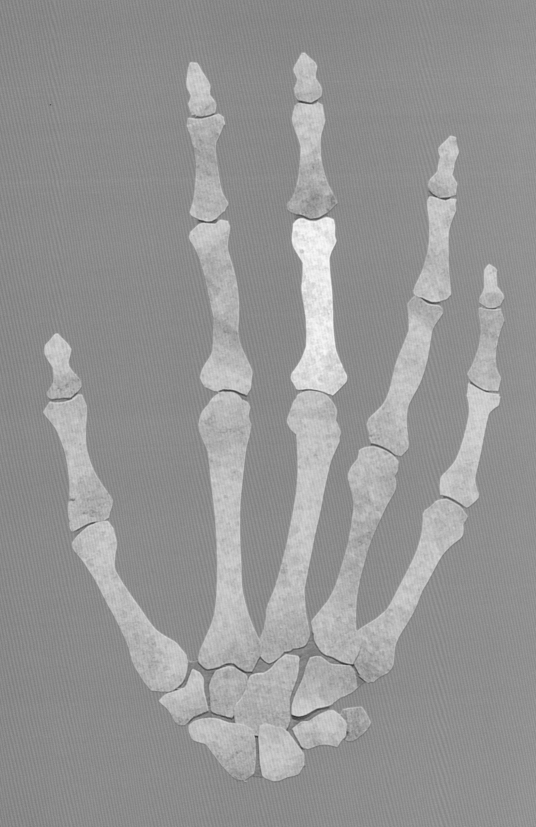

(BONES SHOWN ACTUAL SIZE)

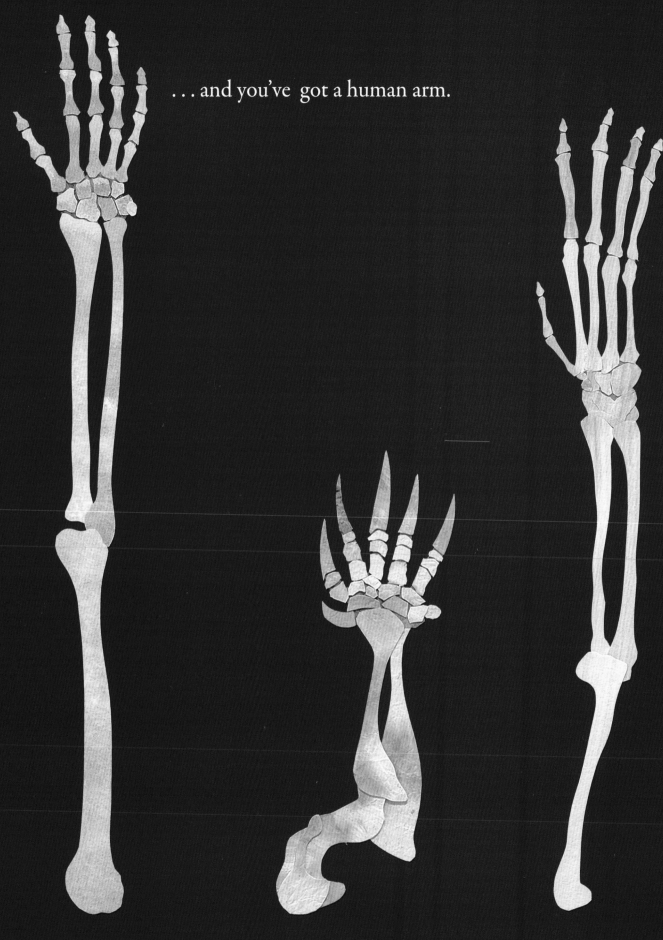

. . . and you've got a human arm.

HUMAN   MOLE   SPIDER MONKEY

Arm Yourself

Animals use their forelimbs to dig, swing, walk, swim — even fly. The forelimbs, or arms, of most bony animals are built from the same pieces: one large upper arm bone, two smaller forearm bones, a bunch of little wrist bones, and a set of finger bones. Animals may vary greatly in size, and they may use their arms to do very different things, but their forelimbs all share the same basic set of bones.

GRAY WHALE

TURTLE

FRUIT BAT

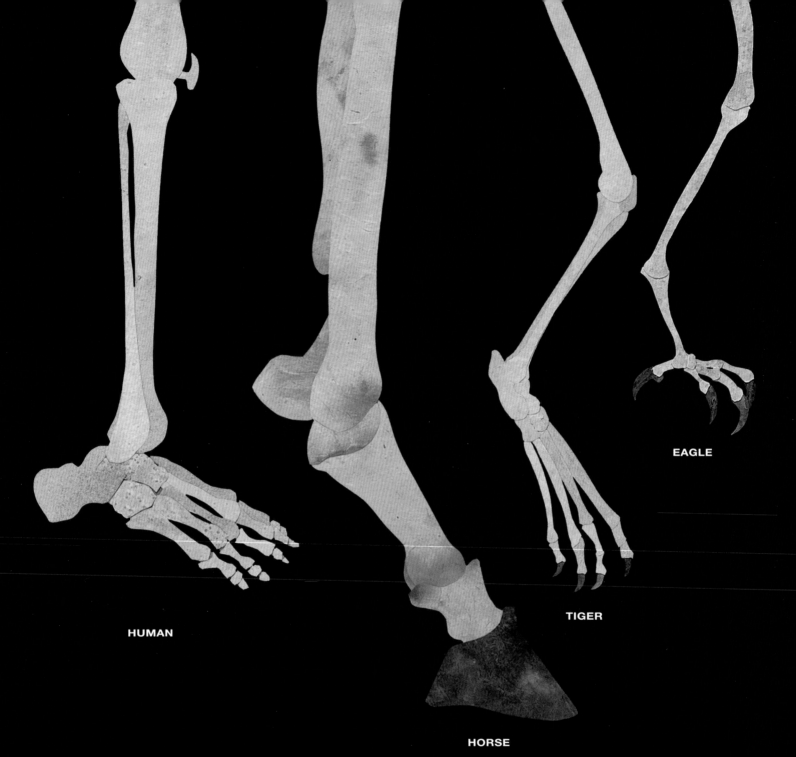

HUMAN

HORSE

TIGER

EAGLE

You're Grounded

Each human foot includes 26 bones (some are inside the foot and aren't visible in this view). More than half the bones in an adult's body are found in the hands and feet. A few more bones complete the leg. The size and position of these bones vary, but the legs of many animals, both large and small, are constructed from the same pieces.

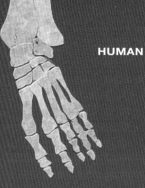

Big Foot

The extinct Tyrannosaurus rex was one of the largest meat eaters to ever walk the planet. Compare the fossil foot bones of this dinosaur to those of an adult human.

TYRANNOSAURUS REX

(BONES SHOWN ONE-FIFTH ACTUAL SIZE)

Support Group

To support its great weight, the elephant has leg bones as thick and strong as tree trunks.

The stork, like all flying birds, has thin, hollow bones that make it light enough to get airborne.

ELEPHANT

STORK

(BONES SHOWN ONE-SIXTEENTH ACTUAL SIZE)

Bony Protection

The ribs form a cage that protects an animal's heart, lungs, and other internal organs. Humans have 12 pairs of ribs.

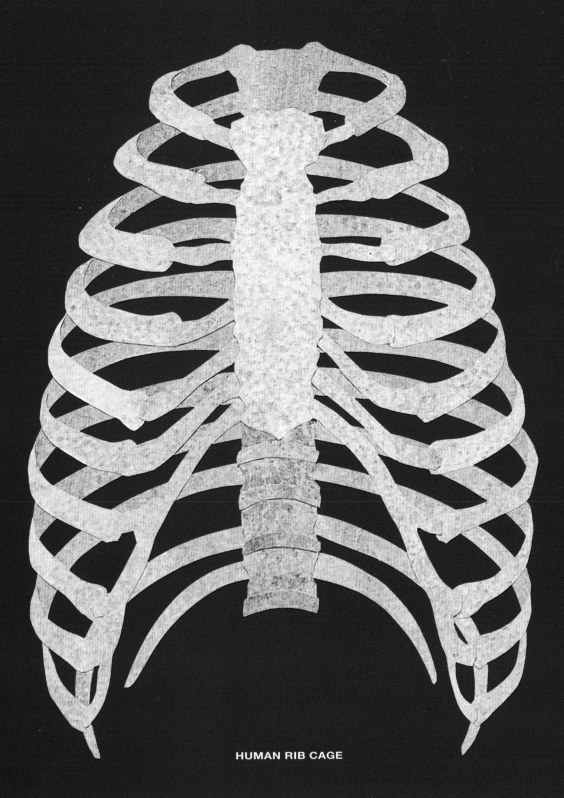

HUMAN RIB CAGE

That's a Lot of Ribs

With as many as 400 pairs of ribs, snakes
hold the animal world's rib record.

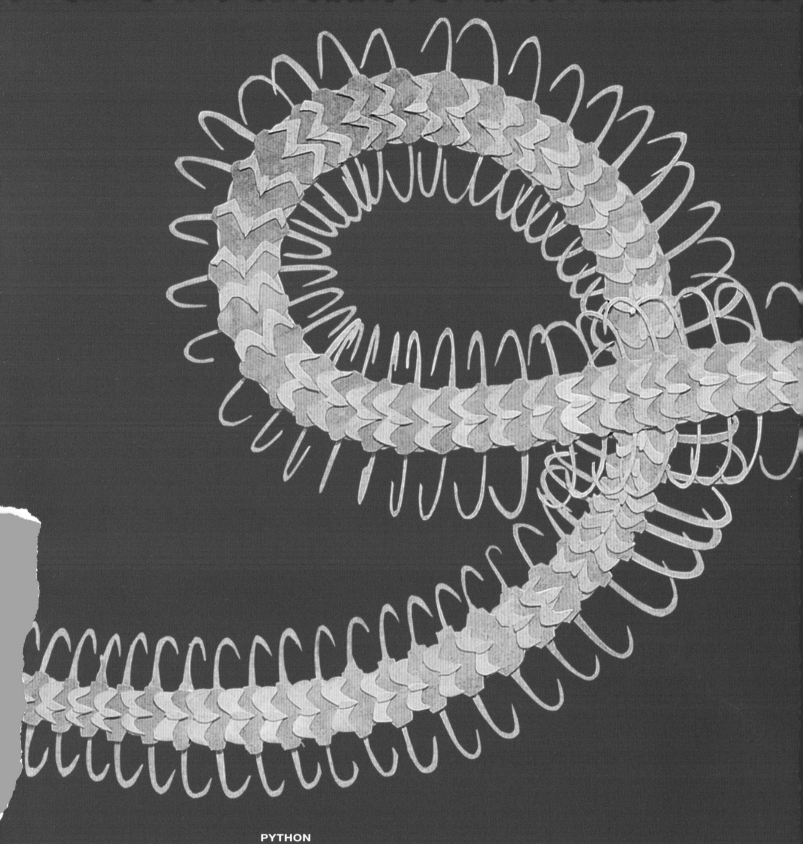

PYTHON

The femur, or thigh bone, helps an animal stand and walk. In animals that live on land, this bone is often the longest in the body.

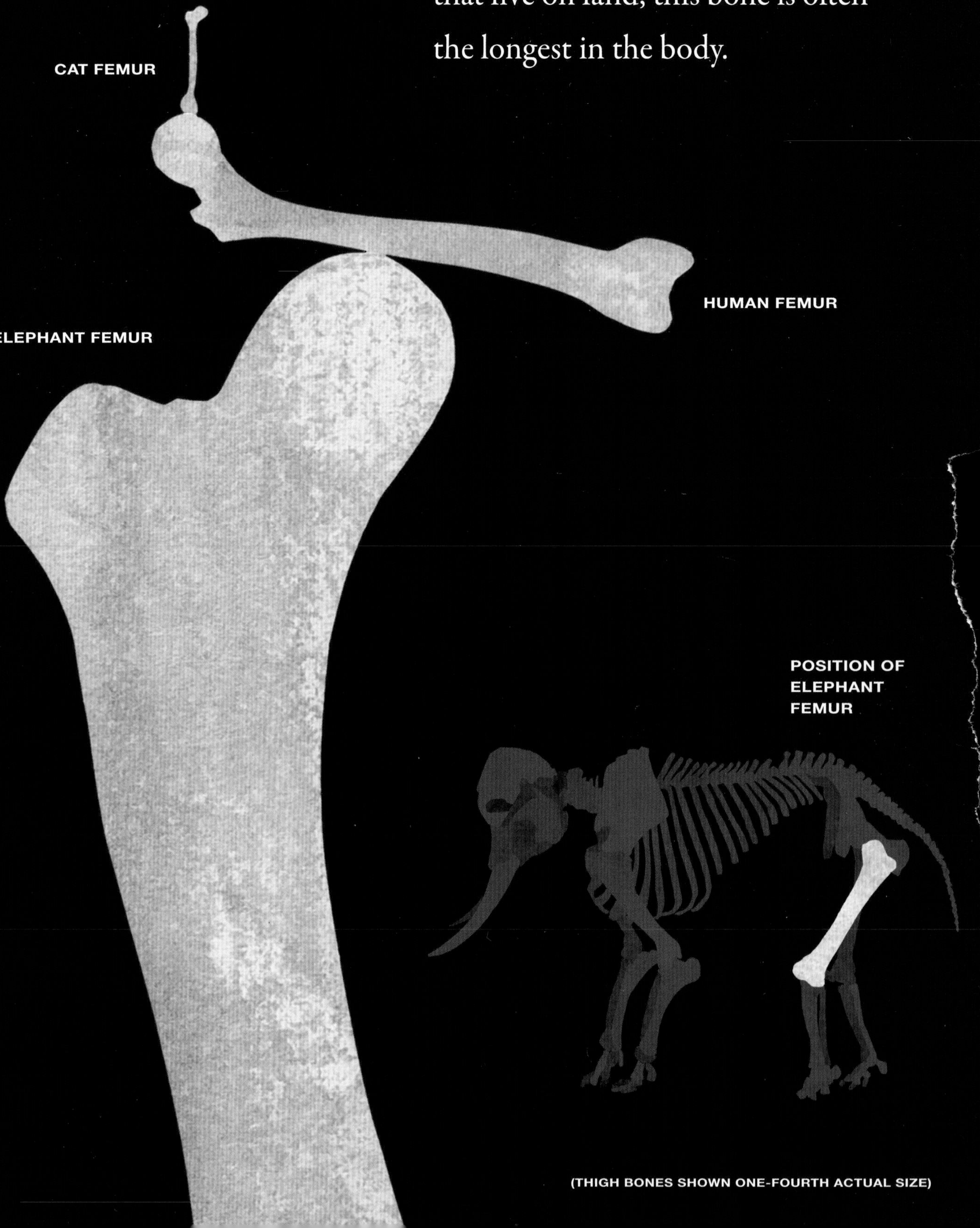

CAT FEMUR

HUMAN FEMUR

ELEPHANT FEMUR

POSITION OF
ELEPHANT
FEMUR

(THIGH BONES SHOWN ONE-FOURTH ACTUAL SIZE)

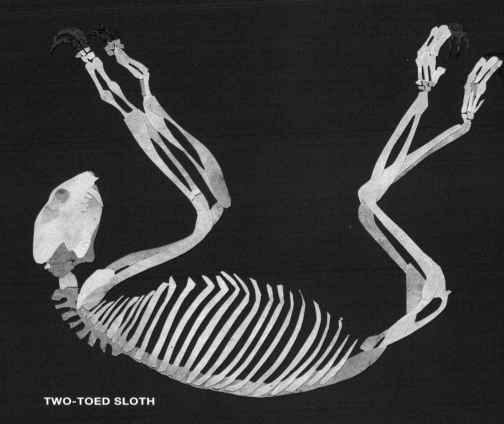

TWO-TOED SLOTH

BOX TURTLE

The two-toed sloth, a tree-dwelling animal the size of a human baby, has 24 pairs of ribs.

Some turtles are tiny enough to sit in the palm of your hand. Others are the size of a small car. All have ribs that grow through the skin of their backs, spread out, and fuse together to form a shell.

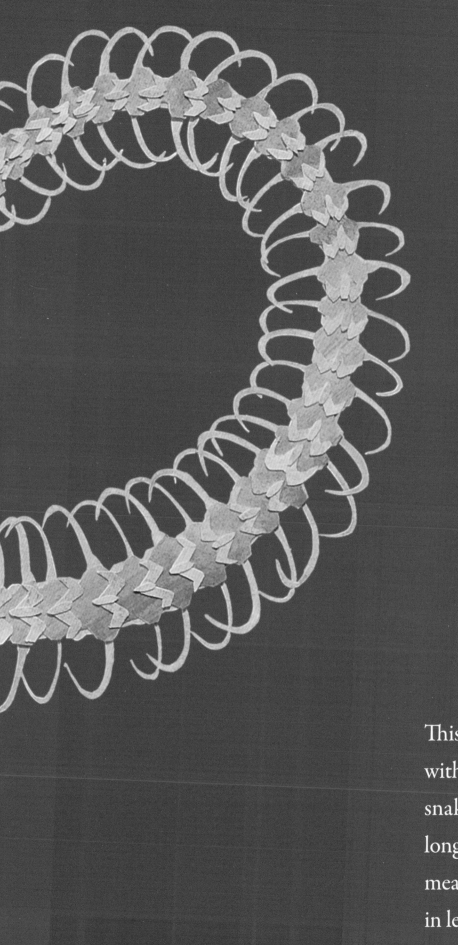

This is the skeleton of a small python, with nearly 200 pairs of ribs. This snake was only about 6 feet (2 meters) long. The longest python ever found measured 32 feet (almost 10 meters) in length.

Got Your Back

Animals with bony skeletons are
called vertebrates. They have a spine,
or backbone, made of bones called
vertebrae. The backbone supports the
body and protects the delicate bundle
of nerves that runs the length of the
spine. The bodies of a dog, dinosaur,
and dolphin are very different, but their
backbones function in the same way.

DOG

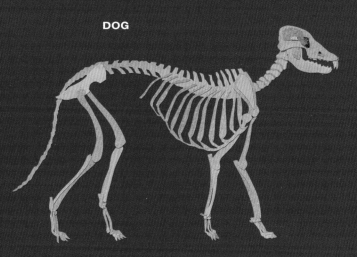

VELOCIRAPTOR

DOLPHIN

(BONES SHOWN ONE-TWELFTH ACTUAL SIZE)

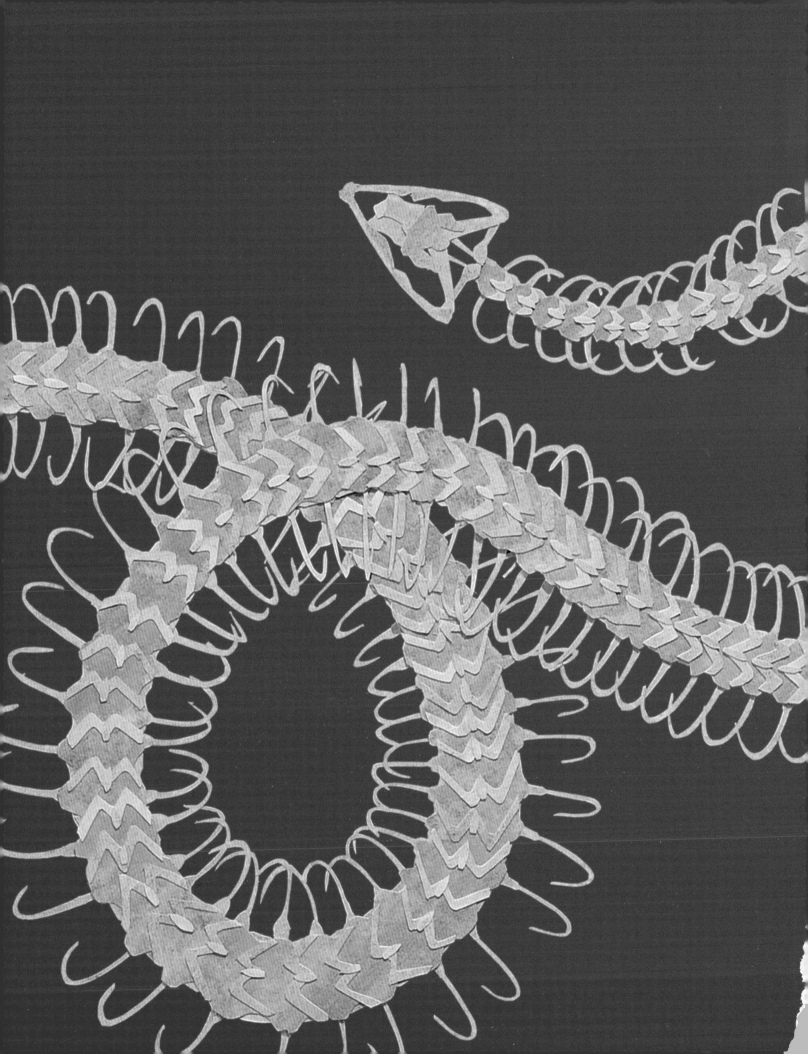

The Long and Short of It

The bones at the top of the spine form the neck. A giraffe's neck is as long as a man is tall, but giraffes and humans have the same number of neck bones: seven.

(BONES SHOWN ONE-SEVENTH ACTUAL SIZE)

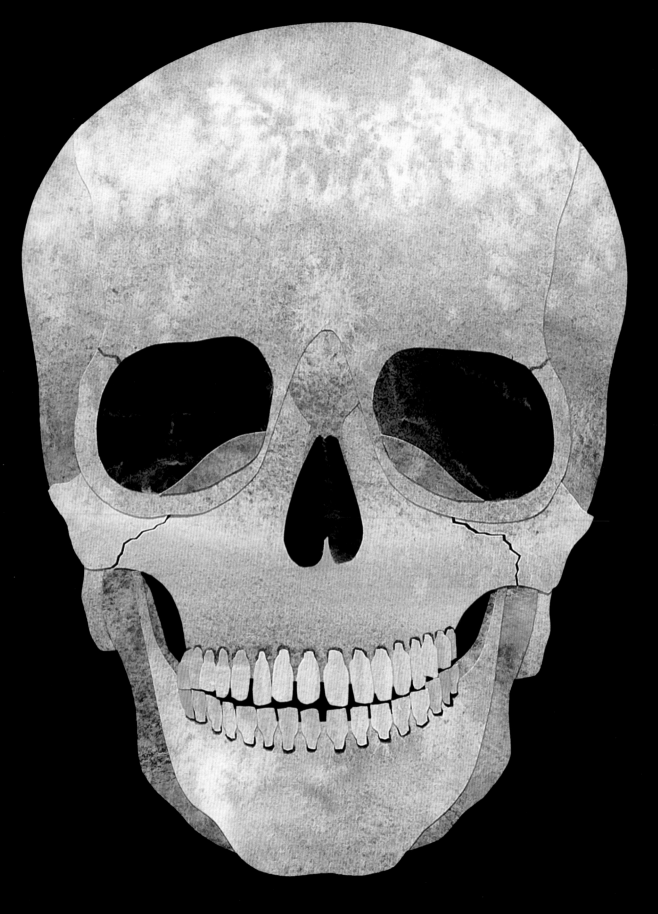

Head Case

Here are the skulls of a human and a mouse lemur, a tiny tree-dwelling relative of the monkey. The skull's most important job is to protect the brain. Over millions of years, this protection has allowed animals to develop larger brains, making them smarter than animals that don't have skulls.

(SKULLS SHOWN ACTUAL SIZE)

CHAMELEON

TREE SHREW

BABOON

BABIRUSA
(WILD PIG)

(SKULLS SHOWN ACTUAL SIZE)

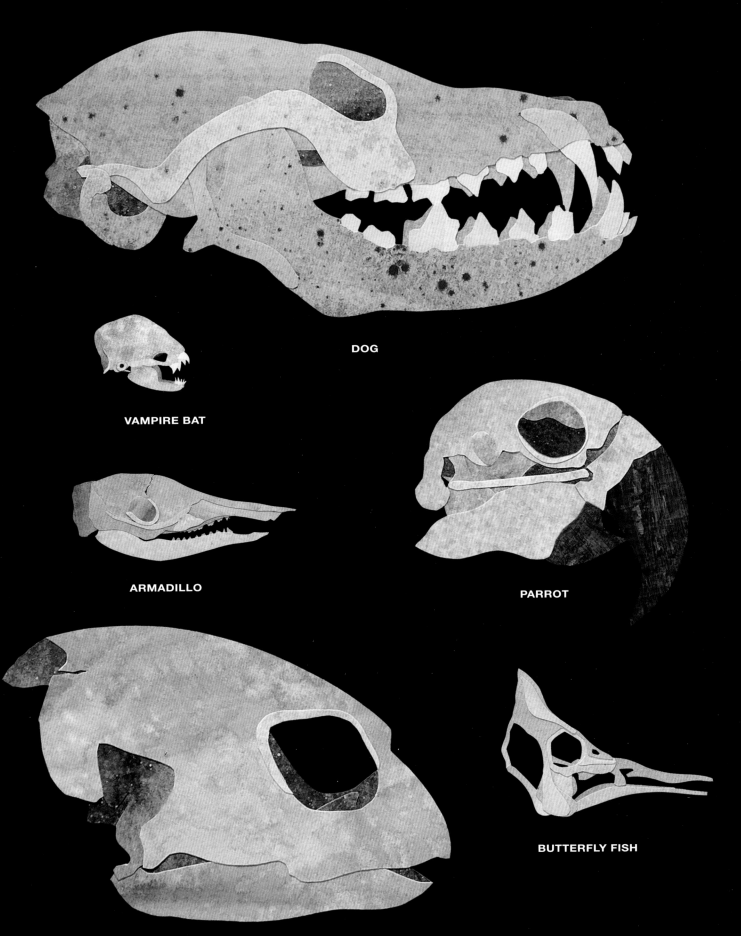

DOG

VAMPIRE BAT

ARMADILLO

PARROT

GREEN TURTLE

BUTTERFLY FISH

Making Connections

A joint is the place where bones meet. With the
help of muscles and tendons, the human elbow joint
allows our forearm to pivot and twist. Other joints
rotate, hinge, or slide. Joints allow skeletons — and
bodies — to move in complex ways.

HUMAN ELBOW JOINT

(BONES SHOWN ACTUAL SIZE)

BULLFROG

Rib-It

Almost every animal with bones is symmetrical. This means one side of its body is the same as the other, only flipped.

Jump!

An animal's skeleton is beautifully
adapted to the way it lives.

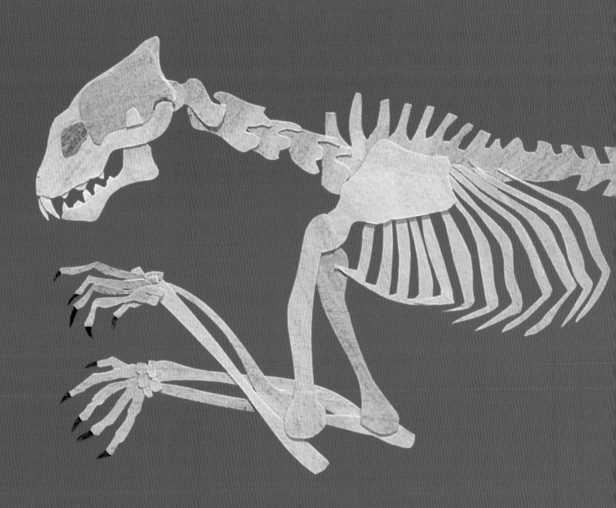

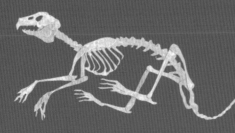

RABBIT

A leopard pounces with powerful legs. Its flexible spine and tail make it balanced and agile. Its skull holds forward-looking eyes to find prey and sharp teeth to grab and eat it. This big cat is a fearsome hunter, but the rabbit's long legs, big feet, and quick reflexes might be enough to help it escape the leopard's lunge.

LEOPARD

(BONES SHOWN ONE-SEVENTH ACTUAL SIZE)

Moving On

A crow can fly because it has lightweight bones. A rhinoceros, despite its thick, heavy bones, can charge quickly. Humans may not be as fast as many other animals, but their skeletons help them run when they need to— like right now!

RHINOCEROS

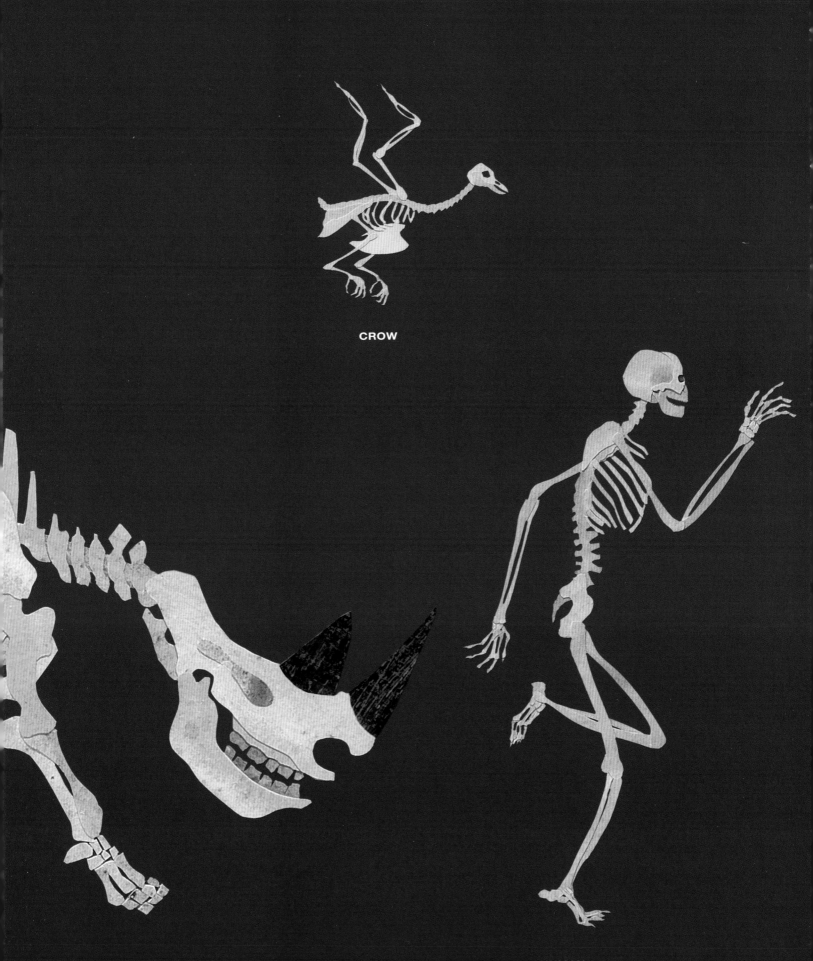

CROW

HUMAN

(SKELETONS SHOWN ONE-TWELFTH ACTUAL SIZE)

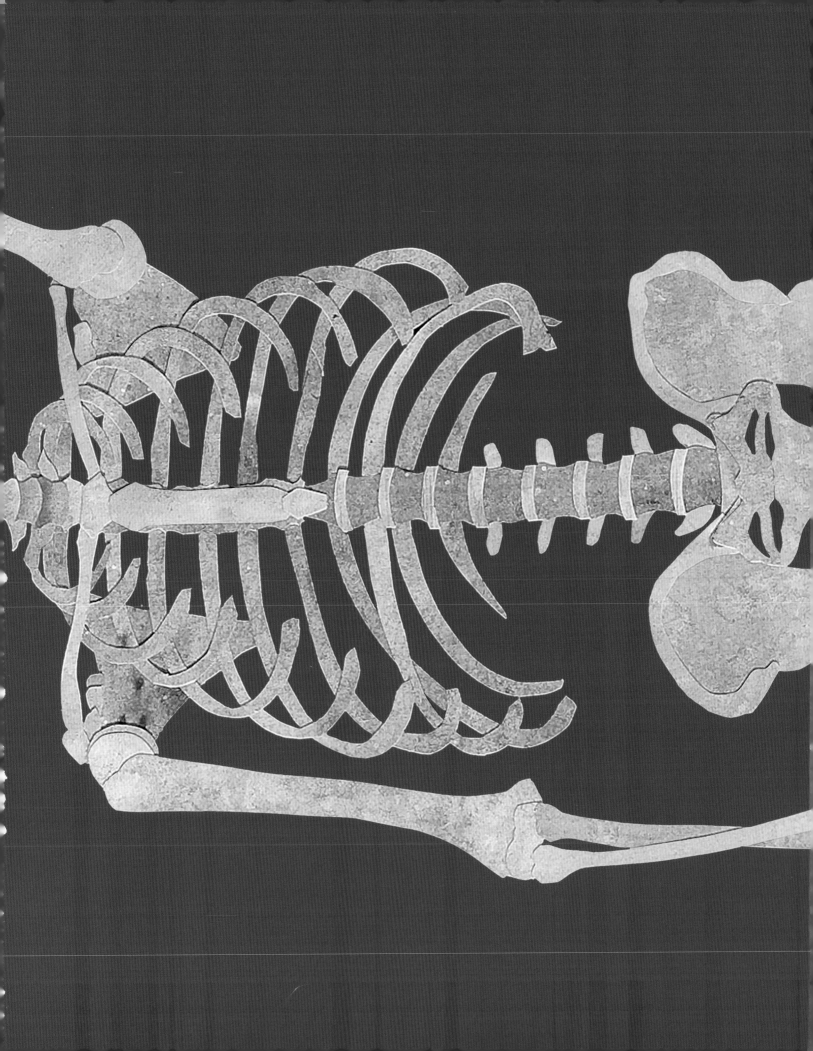

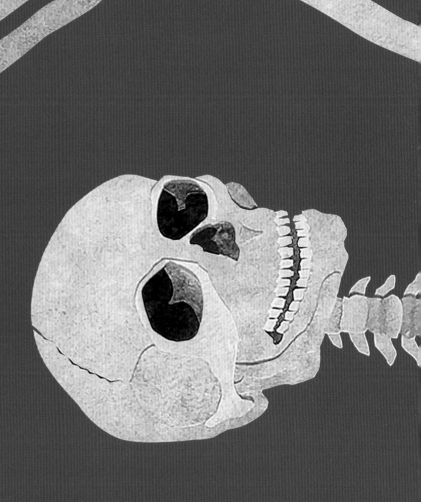

Congratulations!

You are the proud owner of a complete human skeleton!

Some Assembly Required

There are 206 bones in an adult human's body, and each fits perfectly into its own place.

More About Bones: Facts, Stories, History, and Science

What are bones made of?

Bone is a combination of flexible fibers, called collagen, and hard, needle-shaped mineral crystals. The collagen is knitted into a kind of mesh, which holds the mineral crystals. The result is a substance that is both resilient and hard.

Most bones consist of four parts:

1. The outer layer is a thin membrane containing blood vessels and nerves.
2. Next is a dense, hard layer of bone — this layer is what you see when you look at an animal's skeleton.
3. Then comes a layer of spongy bone with spaces between the hard material. This part of the bone is light but strong.
4. Finally, in many bones, is the marrow, a soft, jellylike material that manufactures red blood cells for the body.

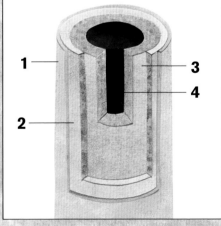

Broken bones

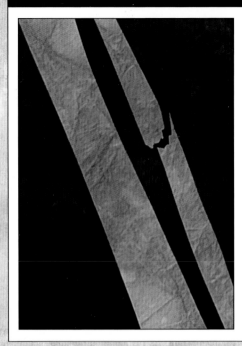

Bones are strong and flexible, but if they are bent too far or struck with too much force, they can break. When a bone breaks, the body begins the healing process right away. Blood cells around the fracture form a clot. Gradually, over the next few days, the clot is replaced with new bone cells that attach to each other and to the original bone. After a few weeks, the bone will be as strong as ever.

The Eiffel Tower

In the 1860s, a Swiss engineer visited the laboratory of a scientist studying human bones. There he saw a cross-section of a human femur, or thigh bone. He realized that the curved layers of bone he saw inside the femur were nature's solution to supporting a body's weight in the most efficient way. Years later, the internal structure of the thigh bone inspired the curved iron beams of the Eiffel Tower.

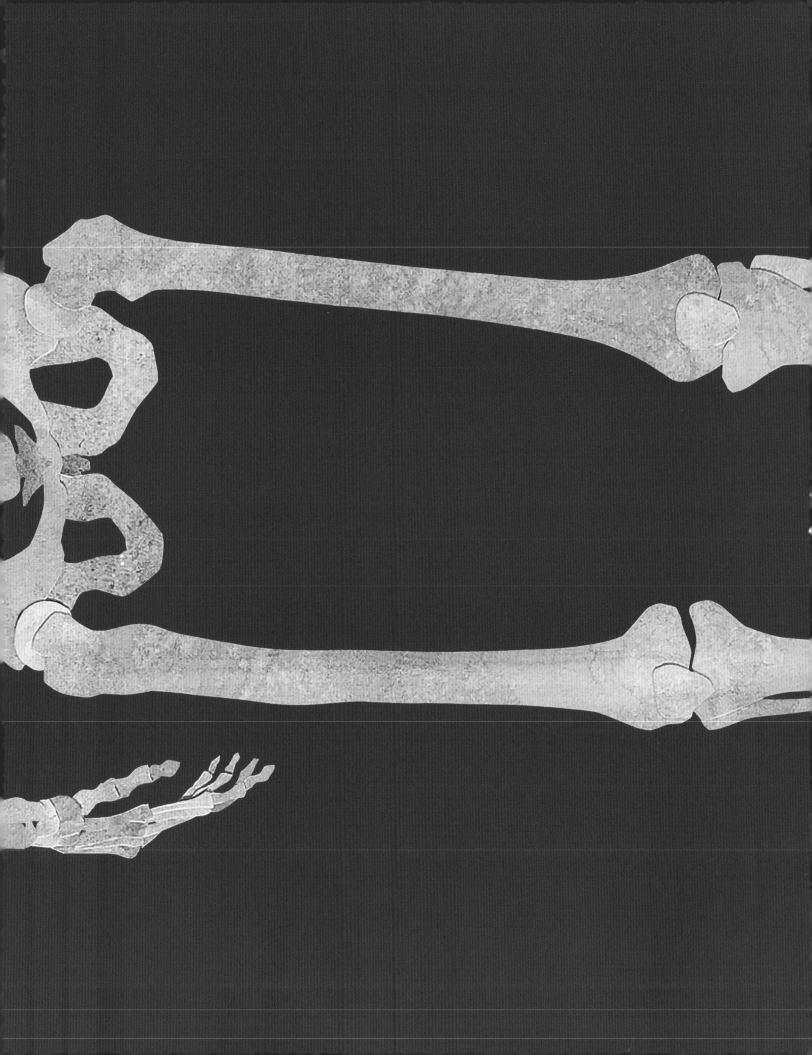

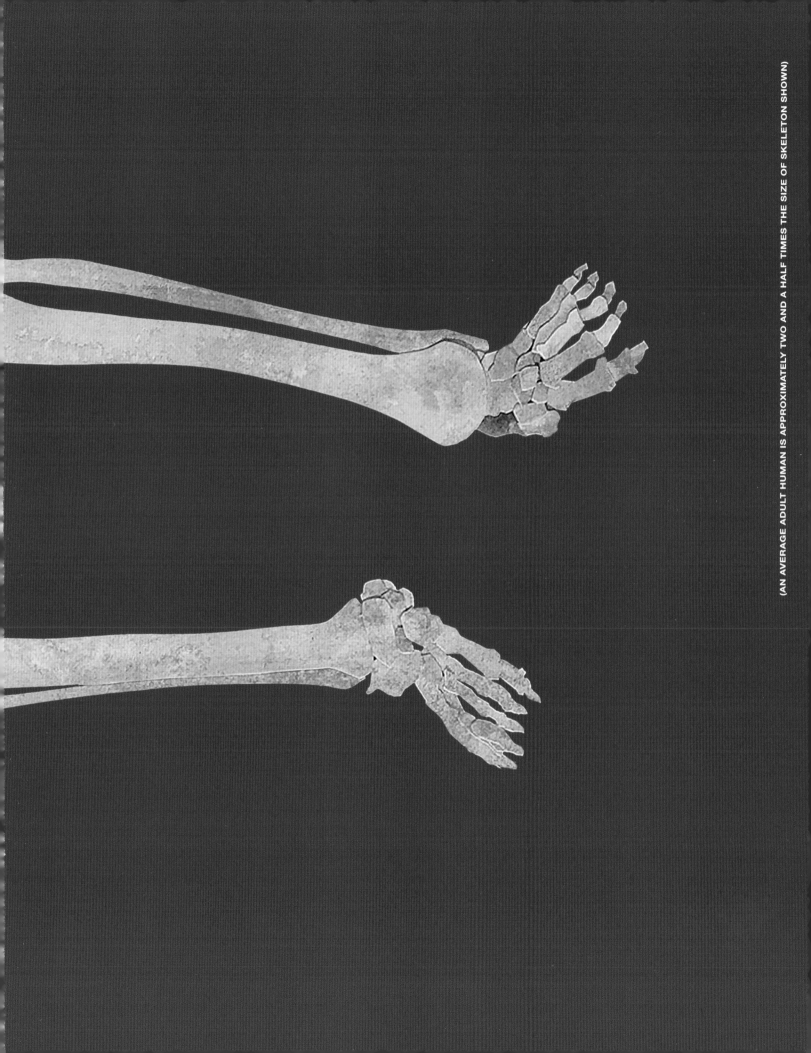

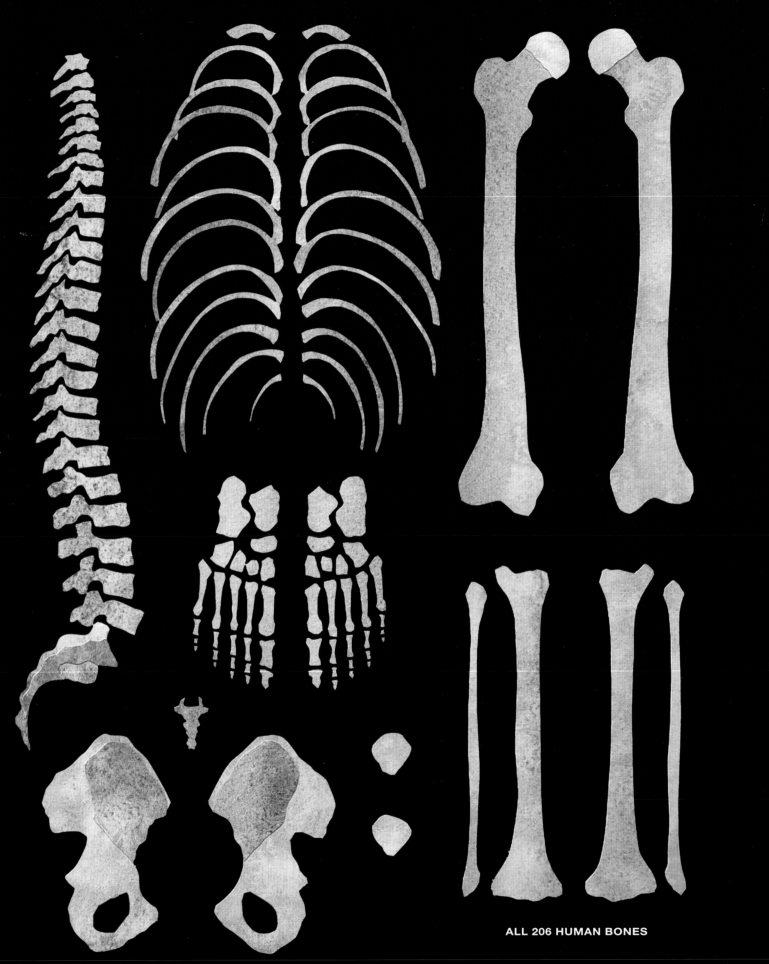

ALL 206 HUMAN BONES

(BONES SHOWN ONE-FOURTH ACTUAL SIZE)

Human bone trivia

• Human babies are born with about 300 bones. As they grow, some of their separate bones, such as the ones in the skull, fuse together. Adults end up with a total of 206 bones.

• The smallest bone in the human body is the stapes, or stirrup. It's one of three tiny bones in your inner ear, and it is shown here (next to a dime) at actual size.

• A human skeleton includes more than 230 movable or partially movable joints.

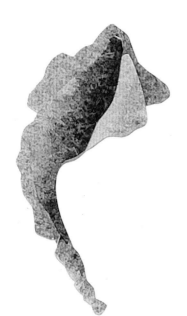

• The human coccyx, or tailbone (above), is left over from a time when our ancestors had tails.

What is your funny bone?

The "funny bone" is not really a bone. It's a nerve that runs to the fingers, passing over the upper arm bone at the elbow.

— ulnar nerve

humerus (upper arm bone)

radius (lower arm bone)

ulna (lower arm bone)

"funny bone"

When the elbow gets bumped in this spot, the nerve is pressed against the bone, producing a tingling sensation – a "funny" feeling – in the fingers.

Cyclops and Unicorn

Cyclops, the one-eyed giant of Greek mythology, may have its origin on the island of Cyprus. Dwarf elephants – now extinct – once lived on the island. When humans unearthed their skulls thousands of years later, the hole through which the elephant's trunk had passed looked like the single large eye socket of a giant.

The narwhal is a whale that lives in Arctic waters. The male has a single spiral tusk – really a tooth – that can be 9 feet (almost 3 meters) long. Centuries ago, some Europeans believed that these tusks were the horn of the mythical unicorn.

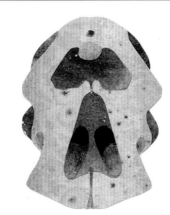

Sharks don't have bones

Unlike most other large animals, sharks and rays don't have a hard skeleton. Their bodies are supported by cartilage, the tough, springy stuff you can feel inside your nose and ears. Only the shark's teeth, made of enamel, are hard enough to remain behind long after the animal dies.

The biggest bone

The largest bone ever found was a dinosaur's thigh bone – a femur – 10 feet (3 meters) long.

The largest skeleton – and the smallest

The blue whale is the largest animal that has ever lived, with a skeleton to match. A blue whale's skull is the size of a station wagon.

This tiny fish lives in Sumatra. Its skeleton, the smallest of any vertebrate, is shown life-size.

A skeleton on the outside

Ninety-seven percent of the animals on earth don't have bones. Some, like sponges and jellyfish, have soft bodies. Many others – including insects, spiders, and crabs – have skeletons on the outside of their bodies. These rigid exterior skeletons are called exoskeletons. They perform many of the same functions as bony skeletons, but they have some disadvantages. They are heavy, so animals with exoskeletons can't get very large unless they live in water. Unlike bone, exoskeletons are not alive, so they can't grow. Most animals have to keep shedding their exoskeletons and grow new ones as they get larger.

Fossils

We know about ancient animals and their bones because we've found fossils they've left behind. Fossils form when an animal dies and is buried in mud or sand. If the conditions are just right, the hard parts of an animal's body – including its bones – are replaced by minerals, leaving behind a cast, or imprint, made of rock.

For Jamie, and his bony knees and elbows

Special thanks to Darrin Lunde, Collections Manager,
Department of Mammalogy, American Museum of
Natural History, for consulting on this book.

Library of Congress Cataloging-in-Publication Data available

ISBN 978-0-545-04651-0

15 14 13 12 11 10 9   17 18 19 20

Printed in China   95

First edition, August 2010

The text type for this book was set in Garamond Premiere Pro and Helvetica Neue.
The display type was set in Dalliance.
The illustrations for this book were created with cut paper collage.
Art direction, jacket, and book design by Marijka Kostiw and Steve Jenkins